Yes, I am Woman!
Poems of Truth, Love, and Expression, from a Woman's Perspective

Presented by Respect the Gender
Written by Anica Walston

Respect the Gender Publishing

To every woman who is silent and cannot find the words to express her sentiments. To every woman who has tolerated and has done the unimaginable. To every woman who has been judged for the choices they made by those who have made similar decisions. To every woman who has cried with a smile on their face. To every woman who thinks outside the box. To every woman who has nurtured the wombs of others while leaving their scars unhealed. To every woman who has loved, and lost love. To every woman who understands she holds purpose and has a vision. To every woman who has surpassed and remains balanced while still maintaining their poise and grace. Yes, you are woman! So hold your head high and understand you are more than a conqueror and your essence is the necessary substance of this world.

CONTENTS

Introduction

Part I

Are you grieving?

White Box
Sadden or Joyful
Ignorance
Stricken with pain
Where was I?
I want
Honesty in the day
Can't sleep

Part II

What does love mean to you?

In the Name of
I blew you a kiss
Beloved Ambition
Kisses and Hugs
Love songs
High School Sweetheart
Sometimes
Your Kiss
Marriage
Decadence & divinity

Part VI

Who is in control?

Introduction

I am not sure why I ever started writing but I always had something to say. The problem was I was not vocal about what I felt. I could only place my sentiments on paper. I had thoughts, which I wrestled with day to day. I had feelings that sometimes overwhelmed me, I did not have anyone to share them with, and so I wrote. This poetry book is about the experiences I have encountered and observed as a woman. As I matured in my writing, I started to appreciate women in a different light.

I have been able to observe the wonderful characteristics of my mother, grandmothers, aunts, sisters, and girlfriends. I have learned to appreciate their individual personalities, uniqueness, and qualities. I have examined the women I have met and were contact with, over the years, and have accepted who they were, even after wrestling with differences. I have learned to value what a woman stands for because I am a woman. There are many instances when women cannot agree or see eye to eye but there is something to learn and love about every woman encountered.

Women come in all shapes sizes and color and at the end of the day, I found that we all possess similar qualities but are also have different traits. We process information differently and we have different perspectives. Some women love with our whole heart. Some women are apprehensive of love, and the complications of it. We long for security yet we sometimes settle for the comfortable even if we are internally unhappy.

Some women put everything first and are completely selfless, while some women refuse to sacrifice for their own selfish reasons. We all possess desires, wants, and needs. We long for passion and completion. Some of us make decisions on impulse for instant gratification. We hold guilt in our spirits in the hopes that it will eventually dissipate. Some of us use our natural instincts in order to shape and mold our lives. While others are clueless and take chances because it feels right or suits the moment. We make mistakes, and some of try to right their wrongs. Some of us are just good natured, free spirited, but lack in other areas, which may not always be apparent. Whatever we do, however we do it, it never takes away from us being a woman.

A woman who intended to capture all of the good, bad, shameful, joyous, delightful thoughts of an everyday woman wrote this collection of poems. There are poems about empowerment, which outline the strength of a woman when faced with adversity. Poems about love that is present and was once held. There are poems that focus on a woman's anxiety, confusion, and her everyday life. This collection also includes a woman's decision of her personal interactions, and tolerances of a man. *"Yes, I am woman,"* is a book in which all women should be able to relate to in one or multiple poetic excerpts.

Yes, I am a Woman!

Yes!
I was released from the womb with the XX
chromosome
I began to crawl and refused the assistance of others
Oh yes, I learned to saunter in twenty steps because
Defiant was my middle name
I studied the alphabet in three different languages
before I learned to speak
I chased mother nature down and insisted she blessed
me every 28 days
Yes, I was a fool!
I greeted acne and allowed it a place for temporary
dwelling, and yes it eventually discovered a new
home
At night I howled at the moon and prayed for an
increase in my mammary glands
I went from C to DD's after 4 prayers
I spewed my first profanity
(kiss my ***, and screw you!!)
Enjoyed it, and made it my second language, they had
the nerve to call me a truck driver
I kissed a boy and liked it, kissed a girl and was
confused, but I liked that too
I misplaced my virginity, wasted it on a nameless face
but he had a wonderful body, and his cologne was
banging!
I commanded the attention of all who laid their eyes
upon me
I used my beauty as a crutch to get what I wanted and
was very proud of it
because for a while it paid the bills
I challenged my parents and followed the rules of no
one,

I told them I was grown!
I disputed the beliefs and the knowledge I acquired
while wallowing in my own misery
I mistook my conceitedness for confidence
I tried to find my identity through clothes, drugs,
alcohol, and promiscuity,
received unnecessary attention,
and didn't know I was longing for affection
I condemned everyone for my circumstances,
took responsibility for nothing,
because it was never my fault
I squandered my life savings on trivial materials,
which can no longer be accounted for,
I think my credit score is…well that doesn't matter
now
I wandered through the valley with no protection
never knowing what it meant to submit and surrender,
even though grandma tried to tell me about God every
time we talked
I was struck down by the impossible and yearned
for more, and somehow I knew I had dreams
I embraced a love that didn't love me back,
but stayed because it was all I knew
I cheated, I stole, I lied, and judged,
because there was no way they were going to get the
upper hand
I was going to bear three sons, and a girl out of
wedlock,
but decided to give them up, only to keep one
I married for security and convenience,
it just seemed like the right thing to do
I divorced because of a black eye and swollen lip,
let me not forget the restraining order
I had no place to go and found a home in
Complacency, on 123 Stagnant Avenue

I began to fight with my landlord Beelzebub, who
insisted I couldn't break my lease,
but little did he know I found a lawyer who handled
my issues
I became tired, and weary, and searched for
satisfaction and read the book of truth
I fell to my knees and begged for forgiveness but
never regretting my youth
I gave it all up never to turn back and found true
satisfaction
I learned my lesson, counted my blessings,
and still remained true to my existence
And though I made mistakes, found love, and lost
through hopeless heartaches, grief, and anxiety,
I took a stand
Some of my actions may be questionable but there is
no doubt
that
Yes, I am still a Woman!

Part I

Are you grieving?

At some point in every woman's life they grieve,
experience pain, and sorrow. There is confusion and
there is pain. Woman wrestle with their identities
while trying to understand self. They feel like giving
up or running away from their current situations.
They sometimes feel trapped. They want answers.
They want a resolution and a moment of comfort.
They want to run away from the dismay and forget
about the decisions, mistakes, and consequences. In
the end, they cant run away from the reality of their
emotions. They cant hide behind their smiles. Tears
are shed, and are very real because when you grieve
you cant hide behind the truth. In doubt, fears,
anxiety, and depression there is a light but the
emotions are there. You just have to embrace them
and express your feelings.

Walston

White Box

So I am trapped in a room that stands still
Padded with fear
The ability to breathe is being taken away
Smothering and suffocating

I become nauseous
As I scurry to find an exit out of this white box
The walls close in

I often wonder,
Am I trapped in my thoughts of being alone
With desperation and despair
Wrestling with time
With dreams that I dare to dream
There is just enough space for me to recognize my
solitude

As my soul cries
For a way out of this turmoil
I hoped to find peace
My dreams of isolation
Is blocked by a dam
Wavering, off the external emptiness and drain

The white box lets my spirit die while
Silently it also anchors rejuvenation in my humility
The white box is justified by the emotions
That can only be traced by my distant heart

I long to leave the white box
With the choice to revisit
On my own accord
For I am bigger than the white box and

It just holds no space for me

Sadden or Joyful

So sometimes,
I feel like crying

Kicking and screaming
Confused and bewildered
Weak and full of fear
Transparent to the world
As they laugh at my lack there of

I feel like crying

Upset at decisions made
Not taking the right paths
Not searching for understanding

I cry,
I was taught, I was fortunate in areas
Of generational knowledge and wisdom
Of elders who held true in their Holy Ghost

I feel like crying

Because today I can't decide
My thoughts are cloudy
And my space feels cluttered

Full of emotional temperament
That fluctuates between sorrow and joy

I do not know
I feel the need to purge and in some moment
I feel that sense of reality is seemingly redeemable

It gives me the ability to express through my tears
My pain to shed my doubts
My abilities to, create joys out of lessons

I feel like crying

Ignorance

I cannot pretend, be mad at anything in this world
I cannot be concerned with visible deceits that have
obvious warning signs

I should not have expected truth from known liars
I should not have accepted gifts and treasures for
returns of lust

My wandering outside the world is no fault of others
My attention too others detail was not my
appointment

Clearly, the yellow brick road was the obvious
choice, but the desert was my path

I cannot clearly challenge known lessons, that I was
taught
Can't doubt the word, when it is tangible and
accessible

No, blaming is not an option

So pretending can be a past time if it satisfies my soul
But the ignorance is obvious

Stricken with pain

She possessed a shield of happiness that was
perverted with a complexion of compromise
and though her cry was silent,

Her heart bled with a lack of determination
A desire to move forward
But a strong hold
To sit in a glary stance

Her body reeked of pain
And the indentions on
Her face were apparent
From the stress of tears
That she cried in isolation

Her fears and doubts
Had manifested
Into the mountains of loneliness
As her prayers became empty
And unresolved

Enough was the word
She mumbled for she lacked power
in her tongue and mental capacity

In a voice that was familiar,
She heard sweetness and compassion

Yes, I am Woman!

That instructed her
To rebuke and release the trials that appeared to
attack

The existence in which HE had created
My child you weep
And I do hear for your sorrow and pain

I can and will bear
For your preciousness
Is helped and can heal your capacity to praise

Even in sorrow
And though your faith is withered

I will not allow you to perish
Just take your burdens to your
FATHER my son
and leave it there

Troubled by the word
Yet she understood
She removed her pointed finger from the trigger

Where was I?

Where was I when the sun beamed on your face for
the very first time?
I was holding you in my arms

Where was I when your cry was as recognizable as
my favorite song?
I was standing over you massaging your belly hoping
your pain would subside

Where was I when your first word began with a, M?
I was embracing your childhood with a sense of pride

Where was I when you wanted to comprehend the
abstracts of this world?

I was holding the bible teaching you Gods principles

Where was I when your cares were pieces of a new
imagination that you were about to disperse in the
universe?
I was their trying to make sure your dreams came true

Where was I when you got in trouble?
I was there disciplining you, and explaining the rights
and wrongs

See I was there, I was there
And in the midst of knowing

In the midst of trying to keep the world safe for you
I overlooked a hurt that a mother should never
imagine

Yes, I am Woman!

In the midst of trying to keep the world safe for you
I let the troubles of my day blind my vision

In the midst of trying to keep the world safe for you
I let unnecessary mental duress wear me thin

In the midst of trying to keep the world safe for you
I let you down

And in the midst of trying to keep you safe in this world
I need you to know that I am sorry

It is my duty and honor to keep principles and morals sustained in our life
And if it had not been for the grace and mercy of God

I would never be able to express without shame

That we as parents are not living in the life of perfection

But we should be in the mind state of protecting the lives that create

We should be aware and be able to let our children know
That in all of our storms God will be present

Cry every tear that has cause inadequacies in your life

But hold onto God
Because we as parents sometimes fail

But when we give our children back
to the living God
that has given them life

Then it is God
who will guide us in our journey of parenting

I want

It is not that I feel alone but empty
And my emptiness compels me to cry
When I cry I feel as though I am drifting

Drifting into a place that I can't see
I am lost,
lost without a path
A path that will take me into a realm

I took the road to the jungle
To the heavens of hell
And I realize I did this
I inflicted the pain on my soul
The pain on my spirit
I cannot write nor can I express the words
I am inclining to do

My metaphoric whatever
Does not catch my eye or ear
I am drifting
 I am drifting and hoping
I will wake up

I want to wake up and dance
I want to wake up and sing

I want
I want
Well that is obviously the question

My freedom of expression?

Honesty in the day

Lord,
I gave up today
I didn't smile
I didn't care

Lord,
I gave up today
I didn't talk on the phone with a positive tone
I didn't share or create any wonderful stories
to shock and awe or even crack a smile

I didn't care I just gave up
I didn't pretend
Even embraced confusion
while calamity took a nap on my shoulders

Wasn't able to discern the spirits
Didn't recognize conviction
And let the devil trick me on the hour every hour

Lord.
I gave up today
Probably used profanity
well of course I did

Walston

Probably told a lie to save face
Well
Didn't think to remember
when I went down in the water
and you quenched my thirst with your words

I gave up today
didn't give a care about others
wanted to past judgment
and make everything about me

I wanted to fight my own battles
Forgot my commandments
And became awkwardly audacious,
befuddled because, I didn't get what I wanted
even attacking fury and sinned

I gave up today
I thought ungodly thoughts
calculated plans just to satisfy my urges

I wanted a taste
and tried to taste
bitter deserts of supposed pleasantries

I wanted to close my eyes
or blink into the distant roads of someone else
I was not satisfied

I did not have any intent on compromising
I just gave up

I wanted to cry

See Lord,

Sometimes it is just so heavy
and the road appears
to far to see the reward

Sometimes I just want to hold onto the easy
where Satan wallows and the appearance
is of no consequence

So,
Lord

I just gave up today

Please, don't give up on me

Can't sleep

so I am sitting in my room
listening to the sound of the silent
cries and urges
wrestle
with the whispers

the depths
grieving in despair
flooding with
life's immortal salts
and so I close my eyes
close the door
to desire

I wish on the moon
for my sudden
escape

Part II

What does love mean to you?

Woman love their children, their friends, family and their companions. Love is the tenderness, which holds the spirits together. Love is joy and happiness. Love is essential, it is a sacrifice, and it is the hope and betterment to women's existence. You cannot balance life without love because love is what separates you from neglecting the importance of life. A real woman knows that love means everything. For a woman is love.

Walston

In the Name of…

I crossed the Alps in the dead of winter
Swam the Nile twice, and survived World War I & II
Shared dinner at the last Supper
Even allowed Jesus Christ, himself, to wash my feet

I burned at the stake with Joan of Arc
Had a dream with Martin Luther King
I landed at Plymouth Rock with the pilgrims
Analyzed dreams with Sigmund Freud

I was held Captive with Anne Frank
Shook hands with Satan himself
Smoked a peace pipe with the Indians
And Herb with the melody makers

My ancestors have beaten me
As I have given birth to an entire nation
I have suffered in mind, body, and soul
I have broken my back for the white man
While I allowed black men to devour my body

I have shed tears for my country
I have cried, until my eyes shut
I have been rapped of my honor, integrity, and pride
I fought justice until justice died

I have spent my life being a woman
And over a decade being lonely
And I did it all
In the name of Love

Blew you a kiss

I blew you a kiss
And outstretched
My hands
To hold your heart

I blew you a kiss
And watched you dance in my glow
As I curtailed my power
To steal your soul

I blew you a kiss
And saw
That your reception
Was to the wicked twist in my hips

I blew you a kiss
And saw you
Glance; stare at my woman hood and mounds
Of wealth
That flowed like milk and honey

I blew you a kiss
And wrapped your soul in bondage
So that it may intertwine
With the likeness of my glorious wonder

I blew you a kiss in amazement
Wondering if
I would ever allow you
To blow me a kiss back

Kisses and Hugs

So I couldn't close my eyes
Without the whisper of your sweet breath
In my ear
For I am impaired with seamless thoughts
Always wishing you were near

I know it is just
Your thunder
That always soothes my rain
Too deeply gaze in your eyes
Always leaves my body in a strain

I think of your warm embrace
That has the potential to
Keep me nice and snug
The bottom line is, sweetheart,
I miss your kisses and hugs

Love songs

If you only knew
That…

If this world were mine

The closer I get to you

You would
Feel the fire…

Soon as I get home

There just
Ain't no way
you wouldn't love me…

I get so weak
cause

All I want is forever

You know I feel like
Cruisin…

Just,
Don't let go
Cause…

I will get all misty blue
and

Where will you go?
if you don't

Give it a chance

If only for one night

I will make it
Unforgettable

Just so you can
Come share my love

Because
You're my latest, my greatest inspiration

So when love calls
know to be...

Ready or not

High School Sweetheart

Short times
That
I wish I could understand
I wish I knew what they meant
I just need to see, because the intangible is ambiguous
The need for security
The refreshment of the new
Embraced
Held
Finding comfort
In something
That possesses innocence
A pure love
No tricks all treats
World free of chaos
Dreams and imaginations that wander
Through
Moments of the spontaneous
Kisses under the sunset
Without a care in the world
But only for a short time

Sometimes...

A kiss as soft as rose petals
A hug with an aggressive embrace
Smiles like a careless journey
A whisper as quick as thunder
Laughter with a three part harmony
A heart full as the earth is round
A hand as soft as pillows
Your sigh a silent cry
A moon full of milk
Your innocence being tamed by some unnatural beast
A soul pouring into a glass of water
Two bodies touching with enough sweat to tickle
Strength that cannot hold weight

A compromise with no foundation
A dream that can only be remembered and remain
true
Moments of happiness like the taste of the small of
your back
A symphony without notes

Wind with the classical notes of Hayden
Flaws that have no sight
A heaven that is not abstract
Trust that has no boundaries
Beauty that has never surfaced
Age that is as delicate as a fine wine
Time that seems to last forever
Sometimes it feels like love

The Kiss

Sugar cannot compare
To the sweet
Nectar
That I longed for in my life
The flowers bloomed and the birds sang
The choir shouted hallelujah
Traffic stopped on busy Broad Street
As Main street shut down

McDonalds didn't have a line at lunch
All the Malls were clear

The Eagles won the Super Bowl
Jordan came back to play

I didn't see the Worlds Series
I just knew it was a lovely day

Moses didn't tend his sheep
Nor did Joseph lose his coat

Babylon didn't burn
And Lot's wife didn't turn to salt

I didn't have an argument
Nor did I bitch about my job

I don't have a negative in my checkbook
And all things are great

Summer is now winter
Fall is now spring

The snow is warm
The sun gives me a chill
And the seasons agree with me

I see life in a new light
My spirit is complete

My soul is well at rest
Ever since, you kissed me

Decadence & divinity

So you smiled at me on a Monday,
I shied away
denied your flirty
flaunts of interest but persistence was your name
given at
birth
and persist you did
Thank you

Cause I held your hand on Tuesday,
tickling the sensations of felicity
and embraced the unknown,
but felt the surety of its rightness

Wednesday, we walked wistfully through the fields of
what if,
and waltz right into the helix of happiness
ignoring obsolete
and embraced the refreshing

Yes, I am Woman!

Thursday, you held me in your arms
Hearts beating rapidly in sync
The eruption of temptation caused a thermal
dysfunction
to my understanding
of what "at first sight" really meant

Finally, on Friday, we shared our first kiss
that echoed the melodies of an angel's harp
as we danced mirthfully around the union
of an undisclosed promise of forever

Saturday, we completed our task of consoling the
void
As our souls collided
creating the perfection of a blended spice
Entangling our soft hues that
Resembled the nougat of a Snicker's sweetness

Sunday, we blessed our matrimony
and its timeless wonder
Our breath saturated with the whimpers of I love you
Causing an unexplained tremble
That would forever leave a "foot print" a
remembrance
Of your existence

For it was seven days
Of sunrise and sunset
Decadence and divinity
A season of rescue &restoration

For he was
My destiny
My little piece of heaven on earth

Beloved Ambition

I want to be held and kissed
Spoken to in the highest regard
I want to be flaunted and loved

Put on a pedestal
Separated from all the riffraff,
And stiff competition
I want to feel important

Singled out and known by all,
Loved by many
Hated by everyone
Due to jealousy and envy,

While never forgetting
One of my many names,
An organized chaos

Always ready for destruction
But closer to God
And friends with Satan

I want to smell the vineyards,
While I sin on the Artic Planes
I want to fly through the skies
And make my presence known

But for now I will sit
In my café and wait to gain, the tools and knowledge
needed to be great for one day
I will be

I vow to you

In my eyes, I hold a gaze of bliss that allows me to
look into your soul
And time stands still just for a moment
I ponder upon what the future holds
I ponder if this is real

For it is the one love in my life
That I was scared, I was not guaranteed

So in my hand
I hold the honor of being able to be guided through
eternity with you
and our unconditional love

Knowing the possibilities of trials, tribulations,
arguments, and fights could be upon us nevertheless
I would not change the circumstances
As long as they are with you

In my heart, I hold the trust that ensures a foundation
That holds strengths and promises fully furnished by
our father
And I know that as long as he as placed at the head of
our household
Then our foundation can never waiver

And with my mouth
I promise to be in a constant moment of loving you
In a constant bliss of happiness
For it was you that stole my heart

And gave me yours
You said no, when I needed to hear it

And yes, when you wished to please me
And on this special day, I know that love is present
A love that will stand the test of time
Just by you standing here before me

I know
I am your current and you my wave
And together guided under the mercy and grace of
our father
There is nothing we can't overcome

Part III

How do you mend a broken heart?

If a woman has ever fallen in love she surely has had
her heart broken at least once in her lifetime.
Heartbreak can consume an individual and leave them
with the thoughts of never trusting in the dynamic of
love ever again. Heartbreak is devastating it can also
become crippling. When a woman pours her heart
into love, she imagines it will never fail and when it
does, she loses faith. Her concept of love can become
tainted. However, women who understand life's
vicissitudes embraces all the challenges she faces.
She absorbs her heartache; she values the
disappointment, forgives herself, and moves on. She
appreciates her journey, the love she has lost, and
knows that being consumed by her devastation is not
option.

Walston

Tonight I lost the love of my life

Tonight I lost the love of my life
Love that I was certain could stand the test of time
You know the love that without any questions is
perceived as dysfunctional

But the outsiders didn't understand
They don't know this person as I knew this person
They didn't feel the gentleness of their touch
They didn't see pass the brash delivery
They just saw how the appearance of what might
possibly be

Nevertheless, I loved him so
He completed my day
Even in the worst of time
My love blinded me through all faults
And even standing by his side
When the days were dreary, when life beat him down
When the cops didn't understand his side
And the judge didn't respect his plea
When women didn't matter, bad habits were obsolete,
I never left his side
Under any circumstance
And even through hurt, there was no possibility it was
deliberate

I had a duty to teach him how to be loved so he could
love himself
I shared Christ and conversations about God
Trying to keep our faith in tact
I loved him I loved him
And even in all that
Decisions and acts have transpired to cause a warp

In our never-ending moments of dysfunctional love
Nevertheless our love

He hurt me, and even through the pain
Do not forget who I am
What I wished for him
And how much I loved

He made decisions
That destroyed something cosmic, unheard of and in
many ways pieces of perfection laced in
imperfections
Nevertheless, I loved him

And for him to make these decisions and be cruel and
hateful showed me a level of emotion that I didn't
think he was capable of
Now, I know he is

Even in shock and awe
I will remember when
I smiled

When…He made me laugh
And completed my sentences and wiped my tears
It is just my heart
The key you held
And so clumsily let it go

So today was full of emotion
Covered with tears
Because even in all that
I will miss you

And I am saddened by our separation

Don't know how to restore this moment
Cause today I lost
What I held close to my heart
I was proud to say I was his woman
Now I am the woman
Who
Lost the love of my life

Break Up

Drawn back in by your light
I soon forget about what was said or done

My heart has every intention of forgiveness
I just need to see your eyes and hope for sincerity

The promise of being crushed far from the ambience
I need my heart to feel safe

And you pull me back in
Sweep me off my feet

Forgetting the foolishness
Remembering the moment of a sweet caress

That relaxes my spirit
and preparation of my moment of desperation to be
resolved

Releasing a Good Man

Despair, jealousy, and craziness
Remembering the mistake of not understanding your
perspective
Has caused me a moment of, miss you
And I didn't realize it,
Until I stared at my reflection
The ugliness of my yesterdays...
How good you were to me
How you loved and held me in high regard

This is my moment of truth
When I admit I was wrong
And you were good
And I was bad
I wasn't like other women who gripe about what their
man would or wouldn't do,
Because you did everything
Fools come in all genders
As well as bashing

I could have been a better woman
With understanding and support
Which I should have offered you instead of the
headache
Of intentionally sabotaging your train of thought
To be a better man

I wrapped myself in the emotion of making you want
What I wanted
And you already did
I just didn't understand

Now I am the one who is stuck in unhappy

Without realizing until hereafter
The happiness was at my fingertips
Therefore, I go on thinking of how it used to be
Or how it is in my world, now

But you don't feel or breathe me anymore
You don't absorb my spirit
Without haste you moved onto where you would be
appreciated
The forwarding address

Oh the disgust of my disappointment
Finally the self-awareness of …
Oh, I miss you

Close My Eyes

So I close my eyes and think to myself why
why do I hear constant whispers of regret

Why does my heart feel like gravity
has pulled it into an abyss of a lost dwelling

And I close my eyes I feel the
the moisture from a clouded tear
and I want to nestle and hide in my intimate thoughts

And I close my eyes to dream of the sensations
I use to feel in your presence
as my emotion no longer can be contained by your
embrace

and I close my eyes to understand the goodbye
as it dissipates with the memory of once loving you

Sitting

Sitting
I think of what was once
You and I
And
I think
That my soul
calls
 to close that yearning
for a closeness
A relevance that was so prevalent
in just a solitary breath
it disappeared
Oh thoughts...
Sent from heaven
 to whisper
the sighs of yesterday
I stare and glance
At the longitude and latitude
of the stars
Realizing
that we are far apart

Undisclosed

I can't talk to you
But
I love you

I can't smile in your presence
But smell
you in my dreams

I can't hold you
But I trust you are
There
I can't hate you
because my heart
won't allow

I can't cry
because
the thought of you
Brings a smile

I can't disregard
for you
will always be
undisclosed

Forgiveness for a broken heart

So as I schedule my day I make plans around the vision and the purpose where my God sees me. I plan to create and foster new ideas and habits that will lead me to a place that will elevate and increase my knowledge. Warm places where the love has planted a permanent imprint of his scent in my mind stay drifting in my subconscious.

A wonderful world would transpose our spirits, so you could actually feel what I feel when I see you. You would understand my emotions, because our cosmos would intertwine. Our thoughts would fuse and unite in just a moment's time.

It is not in me to disagree with my heart and take the high road of reality, but to be honest; the truth hurts even if it is beneficial to your mental well-being. This mental capacity will dissolve, if it is not nourished with a positive impulse.

I know my spirit laughs at the thought, that I let myself go. Nevertheless, this is just another time to feel the unfortunate woe is me. To have the self-made pity party. To think I am the one who is to have a better heart, and be the bigger person. I will need to forgive you, even when I was left as damaged goods.

Therefore, I plan my day around the understanding that I control my destiny, how people treat me, and how I view love. So I now understand that it is not love that you don't have for me, it is love you can't extend.

So I plan my thoughts around seeing the beauty in your heart, knowing fully well you will be a better man someday, for someone who shares your understanding of love as I thought I did.

For I am not weary, I am blessed and full of happiness. I do this in hope that my thoughts and views on love will carry me on in my own daily plans.

The promises to be better, the promises that will make to myself to fully comprehend that until I have had enough, then I will know what I no longer tolerate.

Still love, be happy, be sentimental at the concept. Agree to bare the thoughts of things that you weave into a well-knitted scarf and find the patterns that best suites you.

It will be easier to bare the notions that I can't be or will be found by love
So as I plan my day I remember my happiness. I remember how easy it is to try a little tenderness.

How love soothes DNA in all different capacities.

Therefore, with that, I will love you from a far

Walston

Part IV

What does your fire and desire look like?

Most women are taught that it is inappropriate to explore their sexuality. Her sexuality is supposed to be hidden from her partner and even herself in some instances. What some women never understand is that her sexuality is a part of her. The other myth is, is that a woman's sexuality is always based on love. Women are human. They hold fire in their spirits. They want to examine the fire that ignites in their unmentionable. Sometimes women find their passion in forbidden places with forbidden people. Even though the forbidden is shun upon the fact of the matter is that it sometimes happens. These poems are the expression of women's fire and desire whether they are welcomed or forbidden. They are honest and realistic views for some women.

Walston

7 days to Paradise

See I don't see storms or write poems

I don't fall in love

believe in sensations

or at first site, it is you...the ONE

I don't believe in songs
and afternoon all day longs

staring at you looking at you
and noticing you

I don't do care, share and spend the rest of eternity
I don't do promises and smiles and hopes for the
infinite

I don't believe in long winters
short summers

long hugs or movie stars
I don't do dreams or visions
perhaps and what could
because all these things are subtle disruptions

I just know what I know

I just am what I am and

I am a link of you

I don't need a description or poetic justice

to explain the happenings of now
it is my moment in creation

and appreciation of being
your rib, and I, your extension
Eve content
with you being my Adam

No Breakfast!

I don't want no scrambled eggs
A kiss from you is what I pursue

I don't need no orange juice
My body only thirst to drink you

I don't want no cup of fruit
For just let me be your spoon

I don't want no bacon or ham
For your fat fills my womb

And I definitely don't want no toast
For you are my bread of life

I don't need no breakfast
Just come make love to your wife!

Once Remembered

She stared in his eyes and remembered
when love was new
from the first time
They walked synchronized in the park filled with
the beauty of nature as the butterflies danced
through the dogwoods
She smiled
His hands manly but had a touch of forgiveness for he
knew her past was tainted
but not appreciated by the cycles of dismay

He stared in her eyes and remembered
the bend and bow of neck, her poise and elegance
How she danced through grass as he blew kisses of
promises
To never be the horrors of her yesterday
For his duty was to honor this creature of perfection
carefully molded by God
He saw in her eyes in spite of the tears that often
caressed her cheeks,
softness and grace

She stared in his eyes and remembered
she was his dream
He fought for her in his day to day
as man beat him down and promised him nothing
for she was the understanding
the hope in which he searched for

He stared in her eyes and remembered
he was her dream, the promise she waited patiently to
be sent
To complete his destiny
a dream not a fantasy

They stared in each other's eyes and remembered
the kiss the embrace
The moment when their hearts sang a ballad of bliss
the reality that they both held closely

He, her eyes, she, his sight
souls in sync
His treasure her savoir

What happened

Goose didn't make me feel loose
It was your breath
That sent me into a moment of sensations

Briefly forgetting my priorities and morals
My only thoughts
Are centered around the joy that I imagine
That you bring in, your full court sprint of
effervescent

Herb didn't send me into an empty point of space
I just remembered feeling your nature against my hips
as
we grooved to John Legend
And the repetition sent me into a moment of the
forgotten

Nah nah nah nah….
Your hands on my pelvis
Shot a gaze of true strength that I have not felt in long
time
I felt like a calypso dancer full and free of energy

It wasn't the sweat in my eyes
It was the smoke screen of your skin
That from head to toe I can imagine is all one dark
chocolate …Lord

Being a voyeur was no part of my cognitive
But my aura wanted to watch you
Seductively pull me into your life
Why smelling the sweetness of my nectar

Whew don't get any closer

My English is skewed

Blame it on the alcohol
Or inhibitions
The heat
My people
My brothas
The timbo's
And wife beaters

Lord I got to stay out of these clubs…

Why

Why don't you
Take me in your arms
and warm the night with your sweet breath
that will restore the presence of love

Swim into my eyes
As we; levitate to hire
Plateaus

Embrace my consciousness
and feel the crux
of my forbidden thoughts
of you and me

Taste the sweet and sour succulence
of the vine
that will wrap you up
in my life

Smell the remembrance of an essence
that keeps you in the trance
of a journey that seems not to far
but has an infinite distance

Why don't you express to me what
I have expressed to you and
let down your guard
create untainted perspective

Rise against the power of waves
shield the curses

that wish to
disengage our quest

Why?
Why don't we??
Why don't we???
Take a chance

Lay

So if I could, I would just…
Lay with you
I would want that warm sense of your spirit that
Makes my spirit calm

We could hold each other's hands in our hearts
We could smile in between the kisses of our mind
The ones that take you there
To the place where it is still
As still as the ocean, as the tide rolls away

If I could,
I would appreciate your stature and your mind
which makes you a man
I would adore you and do my best to understand
Even if is just to listen, hold your hand, feed your
spirit

Or just be silent
With you

I would understand
That it would be my pleasure to keep and make you
happy

Because you have reciprocated
The same token
You would be my treasure as I yours

So if I could,
I would just lay with you
And your scent would be
Breath taking

Your body would fuse with my mind
In a state of omnipotence and
Of solitude where only you and I could travel
I know my body would comprehend what it is you
need
Because you would be my equilibrium

You would know my every crevice and curve that
makes me a woman
Things that would enrich my soul

Oh if I could
I would
just lay with... mmm...
You would understand my dreams and desires

As I collide with
Your ambitions and strengths
I just want to lay with you and feel your warmth and
understanding

I just want to be held in high regard
As you would and always do
Can we just lay?

Chocolate Cocaine

My body has been magnificently placed in the hands
of a man
that just doesn't understand
he knows and has revisited my spots on several
occasions

Yes I want him to know
He makes my breath foggy
even when I can't breathe,
Lord have mercy

I need to catch my breath,
as he grabs my nipples with a slight touch from his
moist finger tips

It is the heat from his heart that causes
the sweat between my legs
an has moved to my, oh oh.. giggle ha ha
Oh yes I am feenin,

He straightens my mind
and bends me over
as he grabs my hips careful to spank
and not slap
for the moment of sheer ecstasy …

I don't even have to rub my clll..
whooo, his lips have already been there.
The nuzzle and nudge
As he puts Gina in place
with his bottom lip and tip of his tongue.

And it is magnificent

Because I can now call his name in five different
languages, I need an aspirin or I am going to have
heart failure from the sweat tickling my back,

Oh this can't be this good
Cause I ain't never had it
Am I going to be high like this for the rest of my life?

My body won't accept this,
Damn girl resist, fight,
Don't be the average addict find the 12 steps
immediately before you hit rock bottom

He positions me in the way that reminds me of a
cadence that commands full stands.
His thrusts are so deep my abyss will need to try and
swallow to get some control

No, No… now my honey pot doesn't even know
where the control stops or begins,
he is hypnotic, who are you and what have you done
with my body

That I use to satisfy myself.
What happened to the girl that could hold her own?
That Is now melting before this Zeus.

Oh give me another hit,
and another one, and another..
Oh yes
This right here
This right here is my crack!!!!!

Whewwww….
MY CHOCOLATE COCAINE!!!!!!

Lifted

Let's get lifted
Off the rays
And just gaze
As we blaze
with our mutual smiles
Let's get lifted on touch
and hold
each other's hand
and plan
for the time
as the night draws nigh
Let's get lifted on the words
the bellows of thunder
and drink from the
mother nature's secretion
Let's get lifted on the forbidden
taste
of candy rains
of joy and laughter
of the concealed naughty
as we are ascended to the heavens
and the spirits drop the dews
of manifested cardinal fusion
Let's continue to get lifted
and guide our internals into and eternal oblivion

Urge

I have the urge when I am around you, to smile, hug
you and kiss you, tell you I miss you... I need you to
see the possibilities way beyond the physical, for our
spirits are diabolical, I need you to open your heart
and have the urge too, see I have the urge to see you,
be you, and us together, as long as I have the urge
with you, I feel safe quiet, and protected, resurrected
from fear of not being loved too

See I have an urge, Now that love has taken over, an
urge to purge my inner most secrets to you, share my
inhibitions, stories and visions with you, I want to
feel, breath, smell, and eat from the same plate as
you, make a date with you and act is if we are young,
I feel the urge just to be..

I feel the urge for you to disrupt the heat where my
thighs meet, wrap me in sensations of your manliness.
My spot, where the G lies low and hidden, that
outlines a challenge to all who yearn to savor. Naked
in spirit and truth, I divulge my own, only to you. My
urges that buy into what is, what was, or what will be.
The sudden shakes make me quake and realize it is
only you that satisfies this tickle…my urge

My urges are soothed by your words that whisper in
my mental., your spiritual connections, your love of
God and all his promises, we too share, a foundation
that is unknown by those who do not wish to carry on
through the strife and struggles of you and I, he and
she, them and us, me and he, they don't understand
the struggles of we

The subtlety of our connection allows my
appreciation for the XY in your DNA. My urge, to
call you, follow you, and pick you out of a crowd of
thousands. My urge allows me to sense your
presence your round head, beautiful smile chocolate
silhouette, Tim boots, blue jeans, and fly Coogi T.
No one has to understand my urge but me...

See...I have the urge when I am around you, to smile,
hug you and kiss you, tell you I miss you...I need you
to see the possibilities way beyond the physical, for
our spirits are diabolical...Yes i feel the surge, that
will merge and collide as our sweat tingles while our
hearts beat as one. Why don't you just...
Have the urge with me?

Visualize

See I need you to,
Visualize and smell natures
own way of making your day complete

I am thinking of ways to take you over
and cause a stall in your stance

See gazing is nice
and a soft caress is sometimes needed

But I need my words to gratify your satisfactions
and steal your focus

I want to wrap you wistfully into my mesmerizing
Moments of magic

Flat line
Resume a pulse
and jump start your medulla oblongata

See I need you to
Visualize and smell natures
Own way of making your day complete

I'll grab my black heels and prepare
To tease, taunt, and seduce you

Just watch me dance
as my hips wind
to the melodies of temptation

I'll dare you to try the unmentionable
But I promise you will be pleased
Asking, wanting, soliciting for more

I will be present in your dreams
Stealing kisses savoring the nectar
Of sweet saliva

Your breath will be a scent of jubilance
when you taste my pot of potpourri
My very own delicacy

A nibble on the ear
My locks lightly stroking your cheek

Soft caressing of
Your inner thighs
Massaging, stroking the keys of your success
While your nature rises

Yes, I am Woman!

Oh the melody

See I need you to
Visualize and smell natures
own way of making your day complete

There no precautions, just don't move to fast
Just free moments of ecstasy and erotica
Your wildest dreams unfolding, holding,
curving me into shapes that
compliment our congruent silhouettes

Disruptive waves will drive
the current into a sudden eruption
into my letter V

The presence of your curve
aligns in my center
Finding hidden spots and taunting my equilibrium
sending me into shameful but delectable,
cry outs, of your name

See I need you to
Visualize and smell natures
own way of making your day complete

I carefully close my eyes and clench my thighs
So that my moisture may allow
a more tingling sensation

Small pants of relief
Our eyes meet
and gratified we are

Sweat trickles

Bodies fused
and our exasperated breath
Are aligned in harmony
creating
Sweet notes from the symphony that was just
composed

Carefully exposing our promiscuous tendencies
to each other
But understanding
these are our secrets
Our private and personal thoughts

So as you perspire for the sentiments
and sultry, syllables of sweet
songs and lustful, lyrics

I need you
To…
Just take the time
Visualize and smell natures
own way of…

Me making your day complete

I am

I leave my schedule open
Changing my plans to his convenience his needs
I smile with no complaints
Don't nag and continue on in my daily life

I rectify any situation with complete communication
I show empathy in all varieties, whatever the situation
When I am not concerned
Let me cater to you, are my only thoughts

I give a boost of energy, when there is none available
Whisper in his ears and let him know, he has a friend
Show signs of love
and never mention the sentiment....
Or the words,
Not even once...
once

He treats me like his permanent vision
for whatever amount of time we are allotted in the
day
He feeds me the energy of his soul
Shares his ambitions, dreams, and fantasies

He injects me with an increase of audacity
Questions of the universe that are clearly unanswered
while mentally he manages to find my "G" spot
when it sometimes is a mystery to me

Rubs my back as in a seductive tone
Playing harmonies of joy
As he massages my ankles

He stops to honor my feet with tiny soft kisses
making his way to take his time
to taste my sweet nectar, from my personal secret
hiding place
with the thoughts of it being only for him

He has never tasted anything this good

He appreciates my feminine smell from the perfume
and oils
Illuminating the room with melodic fragrance
Purchased specifically for his pleasure

My feet clinch the small of his back
So I can embrace the heat and sweat that tickles my
epidermis
pouring from his body
He makes me weary with each stroke
as he drowns deep into my love
forgets exhaustion and continues on
as I walk a mile to my orgasmic destruction

He kisses the smile of my belly button and
licks my happy trail as he makes his way on his
journey to the mountain top
to guide his sword into the forbidden city

There is a powerful smile and strength in his eyes
As he enjoys watching his muscle as he enters
Multiple times
He is so crafty that he

Multitask to caresses my breast
as I topple him in the moment of ecstasy

Yes, I am Woman!

Demonstrating his ability to manipulate my love nest
no matter the task

So elated, as ejects his milky liquids
between my caramel thighs
and then lets out a devilish sigh

I dance for him and I feel like a swan
beautiful, yet graceful
or a topless stripper
whatever persuades his mood

I maintain my woman hood and dignity
as long as I permit or settle for this little treasure

And in the end
He still manages to treat me like a best friend
who lives long distance that is just around the corner
at his closest convenience

I bear my soul which he has stolen without a promise
to return
And all my emotions take over
but I maintain perspective
and keep a clear head over the distinction of our
boundaries

I learn to climax and understand my body by his
touch
I learn to fill chills up my spine
By him just entering the room
I appreciate his virile stature as he makes his way to
take over
once again

To fulfill my fantasy
To complete me
To fill the void of emptiness and alone

I realize that this is only for a moment in time
and in an instant I will be the only one lonely
left moistened by an incomplete dream

Cause I am
just…

THE OTHER WOMAN

Part V

Whatcha think about him?

Men, men, men, yes, we love them, we hate them, we tolerate, we sacrifice, we commit, and submit....Enough said...

Walston

He did

He did,
Woke up this morning making sweet love to my nest
and then my body without hesitation or an ok

He did,
proceed to leave the bed only to return with a
breakfast of enriched goodies, to start my morning,
with an effervescent vibe

He did,
Shower with me and wash my back to ensure that my
freshness for the day lingered in his mental

He did,
Assist me with drying my back and making sure my
unmentionables were carefully placed

He did,
Gather all my belongings so that I could be
productive throughout my busy day

He also,
warmed the car up so that the belts were oiled and
lubed, ready for takeoff

He then,
Guided me to my car and kissed me on my forehead
and told me, he loved me

And then HE ......
Took his non-workin ass back in the house to play
station while I hustled for the day!!!

Damn

He good!!

Don't Knock him Down

Don't knock him down
If he sticks around
And willing to fight for the old and the new

Don't be ambiguous or belligerent
When he expresses his care for you

Don't be afraid
Of not being in control
Cause he is taking his position

At least he is trying
And not lying
Trying to create a better situation

And if he is strong
And always trying
to do what he can

Don't knock him down
Or cast a frown
Just let him be a man!

Halt!!!

So if I wanted to be with you and you weren't
promised
does that means the relationship would fail
And if I disobeyed went on my own journey's way,
that would surely lead me to hell

But I am distracted by my flesh
and my flesh is always confused
Between the lusts, sweat, toils
and recognizing being abused

And if I stared at you long enough
the rest of my life would be a distraction
So I got to let you go bro
before you cause another bad series of chain reactions

My definition of a Good Man

He rises in the morning and greets God in his perfect
existence

He understands that his mind has to find equilibrium
in his spirituality before he attempts to face the
debacles of the day

He appreciates his stature because he stands strong in
mind, body, and breath

He greets his day in persistence, for he is always
trying to better

His opinions, respected because his tongue is never
foul

He remembers his manners, ethics, and integrity
And stays focused on his vision

He has and still, occupies a dream
A world that is lest with complacency and poverty

He hears her cry even when it is silent
The disruption in her spirit is understood and never
ignored
because his attention is intended to gratify EVE

He praises her gifts and glorifies her essence because
she is the natural wonder of this universe

He does not swindle, deprive, dissipate, belittle, lie,
cheat or manipulate
Because his mind is set on being responsible for
others emotions, compassion, wants and desires

He wants to connect

He wants to swim in her thoughts
And is effortless in his delivery

He doesn't pant or stomp, curse or behave in unlikely
manners that will disrupt nature's fundamentals

He is perfect in his imperfection
Even if he cannot deliver tangibles, he attempts to
show he is attentive
Leaving the intangibles with more blessings

He appreciates
He loves her more than yesterday
And even in the heighten moment of dismay

He finds a way to remove all cares and be her knight
in shining arm

He is her prince, he is her king
Her unique blessing designed by
JC

Romantically challenged

So she preferred candles and coco but
But the Pistons and Lakers were playing
Oh well…

She thought,
A hug and a kiss on the neck would be nice
he belches
smells of boiled eggs
His nasty ….

Her,
Back is tense and needs some attention
He grabs her in the hopes to get lucky
She says,
Please I have a headache…

She says,
Baby let's take a warm bath to sooth the tension
He says,

I'll be in there in a minute and proceed to finish his
game on the XBOX??
Is he crazy....

Honey,
Let's go out for a romantic dinner and please put on a
clean shirt
he says,
Baby I got some Brut by Faberge
She says,
That stinks too!!

They have,
A night without children or schedules to meet
He
Is hanging out with the boys
Are you serious???

She,
Burns incense to meditate and relieve stress
He
passes gas and forgets to excuse himself
Aaarrrggghhh she screams!!!!....

She puts on
Soft music to strike the mood
But
He would rather listen to Lil Wayne on his MP3
Good grief.....

She wants,
Soft conversations of why love is a just
He
strikes jokes and prefers to laugh at the imbeciles on
the box

Yes, I am Woman!

She thinks,
He is never serious…

She has prepared a meal for a surprise to show her
dedication
But he,
Picked up take out on the way home, but thanks babe
So inconsiderate….

Every day is joyous but sometimes she wants the
special occasions to matter
He justifies his absence of remembrance or concern
And says,
You see what had happen was..
She says,
Oh you just forgot ….and you sleepin on the couch!

She
Shows her dedication wants appreciation
he bellows
aaww girl you know what you do, da bomb!
She thinks,
He don't know me at all..

She gets,
New haircut and a dress just to add a little flair
He,
Glares at the TV and says, look at Beyonce booty, Jay
Z just don't know!! and he never notices the change??
In anger she says,
You really think she would want your nasty
behind!!!!

Then she thinks hmmm
He works 9-5 and flex his time

just to bring home extra

The bills are paid on time
The kids don't want for nothing
And he is always on his grind

He don't curse, smoke or drink
Loves his mama
And can fix the kitchen sink

He tells me he loves me
I never questioned his trust
He loves God and worships and prays daily
And that my friends is a must

Means well and does try to always manage
He has been there through the good and the bad
So why is he just
Romantically challenged???

Excuse the reality

He smiled
Because he appeared gentle

He promised
Because words are free
And were unjustified
With his actions

He smelled
Of cool water

Yes, I am Woman!

That caused fire in
Her femininity

Unlike Jeremiah
His soul was tainted
Spurn with
A closed evil that could only be recognized by prey
he hadn't pounced

His grasp
Caused tension
That crippled the spine
His love
Came with the condition of his lack of morals

His body
Fit the crevices
Of her once shapely form
And those that were
His secret

His outburst
Created guilt in her
Lest his own
buried in her unconscious
Causing fear

And though his power mesmerized
The flesh
For a moment in time
She couldn't help but recognize
the hole that was separating her heart
from her sanctity

Walston

The birds bellowed songs of ruefulness
as detriment was a midst
the banter and chuckles of those who opposed her
position
ran wild through the ears of ugly

planting seeds of regret
she remembered the yesterdays
of whimsical bliss
and yet she wondered
how and where was the creature
God created

She had sold her soul
To a devil that was unrecognized
by naked eye and opened heart

Not understanding why the retreat seemed so hard
she satisfied her disdain with the understanding
that this may be the only love she would have
and a least his presence was panoptic

Nevertheless, she veiled her battle scars, internal and
external
She proceeded to complete the task of settlement
for loving self was but a mere remembrance

Why not
he still appeared gentle
smelled of cool water but a bit tainted
satisfied her flesh by impregnating her with un-
discerned spirits
His smile still illuminated but a contradiction of truth
his words now rumbled with aches and were tarnished
with unlikely colorful metaphors

his actions now accepted under no duress
but he was her reality
he was her excuse

Fairytales

Is it because you open the door when we go out

Or is it the smile at the approval of my garments
It could actually be how you hold on to my every
word

It is also your scent that is breath taking

Because I can smell you in my dreams

I thought it was because of the courtesy in your voice

 that held high regards for my femininity

Or is it the delight in your eyes when I greet you with
a smile in the morning

If it is not those things then I must never forget

That you are God fearing

You love your children

You take care of home

You treat your momma well

You speak gently when necessary

And use relentless force when danger arises

It is the security and unconditional love that you have extended that

Reminds me of why this rib is an extension of your greatness

The compliment of you makes me a better

The completion of you remind me why I love Gods creation

You are my lead and the reason why submission is never second-guessed

The only problem is

do you

Exist??

Cookie

Does he make your cookie crack or crumble?

Does he lie or does he cheat

Does he make your cookie crack or crumble?
Going back and forth, arguing even in defeat

Does he make your cookie crack or crumble?

His laziness and omission of sins, that causes you to gain weight

Does he make your cookie crack or crumble?

Holding on to what is left of your mental state

Does he make your cookie crack or crumble?
While you always contemplate throwing him out

Does he make your cookie crack or crumble?

Then you realize you're dick-matized, and all those tantalizing shouts

Does he make your cookie crack or crumble?

You know his misery causes so much pain

Does he make your cookie crack or crumble?

I know this is the third time you took him back

THERE YOU GO AGAIN!

Did you like me?

Ummm… did you like me?
Cause you didn't call me

And you said you would
You told me you had a good time
And I thought that maybe just maybe you and I
Could do it, one more again

I know, I know
I never do that on a first date
But you were so kind
How you wined and dined me
I never knew that flamed broiled could be so-so tasty
And I am cool that we split the combo because you
trusted me to drink out of your
Straw
And we even got free refills
That was the best!

I know my tank top and big old thighs mesmerized
your eyes
and you virile stature just made me weak
That is why I need to know
Did you like me?

Cuz I know that room wasn't cheap, economy and all,
and it even had a microwave
It was a weekend day and you have a home to go to
But you…wanted some privacy
Cuz yo mama was off work, and you didn't want to
be disturbed
So I knew you thought I was special

And it was alright that your homeboys came through
to smoke a bogie or two
Cuz men that are trying not to be tied down don't
introduce a lady unless it is their potential baby
mama, call me crazy but…
 I just knew, I just knew

Cuz no man has ever took his hand and the time for
me to see
not one but three movies
Even if it was the hook up, 3 for 5
It was the latest releases and you know it will be
months before they come out on DVD
Forget on demand because our lands expand and hold
much more value with the time you showed me

You really cared
Even if I just met you this afternoon
And I want to say thank you
Because I think, you liked me

The very thought of you offering a massage to my
tense body was ever so kind
It was my first time and you made me feel special and
needed
You made me feel un-shy to show you my personal
places where no one's faces ever
stop and venture,

Even though I know you don't like to kiss
aww man you are so awesome
It is alright that you forgot a condom

Then we lay there and cuddled
Although I was holding you

You didn't mind and in time you fell fast asleep in
my arms
or was that me who fell into dream land
I can't recall because after that drink
I could hardly think I just knew it was a night to
remember

But when I opened my eyes it appears that you
already had rised
And I missed the morning to greet you with a smile
Show you my gratitude
and kiss the sun
But I understand you're a business man
So you probably had to make a run

But now it's been weeks, and I am still in a daze
Cuz my black berry hasn't buzzed or beeped

You have been on my mind and I see your face pop
up a thousand times
And I would understand if you didn't want to get to
deep
But my doctor said in a few months I will be dead
Cuz… I have contracted a strand of HIV

So I was wondering if my blunder was in vein
If you feel the same cause
I just need to know
Did you like me?

I apologize

So I apologize…
For being a woman of true essence that stands beside
her man through thick and thin even when the lies
began
and the tainted truths are disguised by the moan of
pretend
when you attempt to make love

You are mentally limp, and I apologize because I do
not excite you but incite and dare you
to see, using the image of greatness
I know I throw my education around and articulate
artistic abbreviations that echo sounds of a possibility

Even in hard times, I know I complain because being
a black man may cause bitterness, bewilderment, and
belittlement just because of your skin
And I don't understand the struggles of your day to
day
Because I am not you, and I have work to do

I apologize…
Because I thought, it was the weed smoke and pint of
Hennessey that caused you to philosophize
and find every decline and deceptions in this
"conspiracy theory," that was holding you back like
cardiac failure clogging your arteries and shutting
down your vital organs
Filling your lungs with fluids that cause you to drown
out what and who you were meant to be

 I apologize…That I don't

Listen to your chants of ignorance and excuses to
why the man is holding you down
When it Is apparent to me
 that
I see your controller's keep you tide to the TV, while
you masturbate to ESPN, and hope the Lakers win
Collect a ring but you see they have a dream
and a check is common to their day to day living..
my bad
I forgot you were sensitive

So I apologize…
Because I wasn't aware of my place since I seem to
always be up in your face, and for better or for worse
were just some words we said in front of a judge
before the notion of until death because a reality and
a headline on the 11 o'clock news

I need not say another word and began the process of
release
Because I am cold and bold and my tolerance has
now been limited to an ultimatum
You see it is better for you to be free because you
don't need someone like me
Always causing confusion and tension and other
things I dare not mention

So free you will be because you don't need me
And you probably should have read all of my
credentials
So my bad homie
Cause I apologize…
For believing, you had
Potential!

Part VI

Who is in control?

Yes, we are women and we have power. We have a right to embrace who we are. We have a right to our confidence. We have a right to make mistakes. We have a right to feel joy. We have a right to be who we are supposed to be. A woman should exude confidence and strength. A woman can be selfish and selfless. A woman can be arrogant, a woman can be standoffish. A woman can be kind, moody, and humble. Why, because she is a woman. If women did not possess all of these qualities then a woman would not be able to mother a child, run a corporation, make cookies for her child's afternoon activities, hold a position in a high office, take on challenges that are unheard of, leap mountains, break barriers, stand at the head of her household, and stand beside her man if one is present.

Walston

Not

So if you are looking for an equal you're not looking for me

I don't do taking out trash, cutting grass

Washing cars

Handy work

Pulling tools

Be your father

Gathering in small group ogling at girls

Scratch my personals

Pat others on the butt

Spit on concrete

Hide my emotions

Work construction or other hard labor

Lie because I scared of the truth

I am not a man, transgender, nor do I hold the XY chromosome

However the house will be cleaned, the children will be well kept

You will be fed the breakfast, lunch and dinner fit for the King that you are

The finances in impeccable order

And as my man no complaints about my attention to your body in detail will ever be an issue

My love will always be forthright

And I will not compromise or tolerate anything outside of my expectations

I am not hear to compete but to compliment

Handle your manly duties and

There is no question

That

I will always be and am

A WOMAN!

Play List

My play list is so tight
 it is specially tailored
 to my sentiment and value of how high my
Moments of romance and faulty relationships build
 It amazes me
That even in crisis
My play list made a way for new feats of
understanding
To enter in sporadic moments of the day

I understood that Karen didn't want to be a "Super
Woman"

But confused me when she said in the same breathe
"I'm your Woman"

Roberta was trying to get me to remember the
 "First time I saw your face"

Mariah forgot that I needed
to hold my composure
And just let me "Melt away"

At the site of your virile mystique
that waiver the molecules
from exploding
causing a disruption in my nervous system
and then I realized

"U know how to love me" Phyllis told me
and I couldn't get over

How much you were my "Angel"

Thank you Anita
When the battle got tough

I knew "Through the fire" Chaka was going to pull
me back
into reality even though
I lost perspective

But I paid attention to Escape when they told me your
"Eyes may tell me secrets"

So I wouldn't be shocked or disappointed
in the trust that you dissipated
And the memories of the "Love that should have
brought you home"….mmmm Toni

Will never drag me to hell
Trust, I still had Love…
"Long after the love lost its shine," Regina explained

Because I was not going to travel the roads and
questions of
Where do broken hearts go...Saddening Whitney?

So what I did was make me a new play list
That was more attainable to my fire
to get my point across
And stand up for who I believe in

I wasn't
belting out "If Ain't got you" Alicia

Cause in your twists and turmoil
I realize that my play list
Described the fight that my other

Sistah's struggle with daily

So when I feel bound by what could have
or should have been
I remember who I am
and what I did with you

You got me twisted!

So I say
Thank you
Beyonce
He must not know bout me!

To the left to the left
cause
I don't ever need you to think
You are "Irreplaceable"

Time for a new play list!

Superego

In the jungle
I soak my roots for growth
I prepare a righteous meal
To feed my soul
I walk on water
So my feet are never dampened
By the filth that tread it
I assume I will never age
For I am a flawless man
I was born a righteous leader

With magnificent power
I am stronger than Superman
I have the influence
To control your ups and downs
I see you yearning for me
I have the ability to make you cry
In fact some fear me
I feed off your destruction and chaos
Fairytales and fantasies
I create your personality
I execute you
Hold your flesh hostage
And sometimes I mean you know well
My intent has caused eruptions in your faith
For just common nature
I am deadly
If you are weak
I am you

Options

I need to hear the sounds of creativity
running through my veins
Pumping blood in my brain
To illuminate my imagination

I need a song
that plays over and over again in my head
Without the repeat button on a CD player
Finding the notes
And understanding the purpose of the treble clef

I need a cool drink of water
So that the heat can absorb into

my outer epidermal layer
While I perspire my cares away

I need my child
to tell me a joke that I don't understand
but will laugh because it will make his day
and smiles are priceless

I need a cook out
With burgers, hotdogs, ribs, chicken and fish
because I eat all meats
that won't eat me
and I believe in survival of the fittest

I need the negative
so I can find the positive
and express my incite to the betterment of me
while rebuking Satan for his attempts
on my faith

I need a high that
doesn't come from a laboratory
is not home grown or chemically induced
Because
My mind should be freed by mother natures
Mystic melodies

I need an alter ego
Who is not shy
That no one knows
And everyone wished they knew
Because in reality it is really me

I need a definition
And a plentiful vocabulary

To understand new words and form clauses
because
Wisdom is what I want to retain
And it is knowledge that I seek

I need a walk
To exercise my rights
And freedom to just be
A woman
And birth milestones
 to shape history
Pure and full of peace

I need a pen to record my thoughts
And share my descriptions
Of the sun, moon, stars
Bridges over shallow waters
capturing
Possibilities Of what if or why not

I just need
For you to feel me
And appreciate my presence
By opening up your minds
To newness and endless
Constructive concepts

Carefully folded in my cognitive

I just need you to need me

I wanted to write a poem and express ….

I wanted to write a poem and express ….

I wanted write a poem and show you new ways to
encounter your consciousness
I wanted to tell you a story about the yesterdays
The days of whenever and wherever

I wanted to debate on some topics and look to agree
to disagree

I wanted to dance as if I was at a VSU, Jim-Jam
and just remember hip hop
when it was really hip and less hop

I wanted to be free and skip with my best friends and
tell secrets and lies about what we wanted to be
what we were doing
and who we were doing it with

I wanted to take a ride down Sycamore and envision
our history
on the way to Old Towne
where they sold my ancestors

Eat at the French Besty where I suppose
I would enter the back door in order to be served

I would like the commonwealth not to be so common
in there hypocritical laws and disdain for the human
capacity

Walston

I would like to travel consciousness and conclude that
ignorance is the stagnation of a people who choose
not to work together as other groups

I wanted to write a poem and express
Share what I think about when I am pondering what
to record next
in my notebook of imagination

I would like you to see the colors that I feel when I
smile at glory, mercy, and forgiveness

Appreciate with me the sun and the moons which are
housed in this universe of omnipotent creation

I just want to think
And be allowed to do so without being enslaved in
my own adaptations of following the unrighteous

I want to be led by God
and be a leader of new ideas

I want to share and think out of the box with my
sisters and brothers
Because in our struggles comes great inspiration and
creativity

So as I write
visualize your moment of greatness
Remember your good and bad yesterday's
Remember to love
remember to be free in your cognitive abilities
the only reason to be in bondage is if you hold

yourself captive in others reality

So maybe it is not a poem just my expression

Searching

I am color blind and tone death

Without the salt and sugary taste

in my mouth,

I am present, and cannot be seen,

I am a lie that only seeks the truth,

I am a mother without the wound
to bear a child,

I am a soldier who cannot find
the battle ground

I am a writer
that cannot read nor spell
the emotions of my heart,

I am a teacher that has not
organized a lesson,

I am a doctor
who has no Ph.D.,

I am a queen

who lost her land to the world of chaos

I am a mystery never solved,

I am a glass of water half full,

I am a fool without his tricks,

I am a player without
my kicks,

I am a martyr
that wished to be known while alive,

I am a man with no courage
who once stood six feet tall,

I am alone with no identity,
and one who is still searching

Sisters

Are like the end of a rainbow
A pot of gold
A treasure
Of unique blends
Carefully mastered
and orchestrated by God
For you are symphonies
Full of notes
That has harmonious joy
You are a friend by force

But you never mind at all
You are a groundbreaker
that breaks new ground
And leads a path for those to follow
You are a gift and blessing
that everyone is not privy to
Your beauty reminds me
of a glance of my beauty
For I am an extension of you
You rise
for you know
that your intangibles
are wrapped in your faith
You are, and will forever be
in my delight
because you are a piece of my spirit
Your willingness to pursue
and leap unthinkable boundaries
are always in eye's view
This is the day that you are adored the most
for without this day
You would not exist
So I thank God for creation
I thank God for conception
For you are a natural being
full of bliss
For you are my sister

Word Play

So I close my eyes and carefully calculate
a new construction of the chaotic cosmos
which renders to my mercy, when my power is
present

So I don't see real, I am real
As real as reality gets
when is restored and re-captivates your readiness

But I shan't not whisper
cause I need you to utilize the vigor and voom,
while the vivacious vixen, rests her verbs, on various
adjectives

So please pardon me
for my purpose is not to play, politics, people or
personas
But to push, pump, and pulsate, some new blood into
your veins

Like an IV, holding saline to saturate the very
substance that secures your
Selflessness

See words are witty,.. written, when we seek a new
description
an explanation of what we believe is a wavering
mystery

So I dare not assume
that you lack understanding

of this list of lyrical lyrics, full of metaphors and
myths
that sometime manifest into our own mystic

It is my word play,
it is a path to my spoken, sporadic, spontaneous
words
that should leave you smiling, speechless, and
satisfied

Conforming ...Right ?

So my ladies are always trying to conform
to what has been decided to be acceptable
but I say .. hell no !
Cause I was born the way God intended

I have this hair because it is an extension of my
power

And it's coils show the extension of my true roots

I have these lips so I can kiss and breathe life back
into those lost souls

You see I have these hands

So that all can come share my love
I have these breasts to nurse the land
and please my man

I have these stretch marks to show the proof of being
able to bear the souls of this universe
Not ashamed at all, kiss them or kick rocks

And these hips are for rocking back and forth to any
groove I feel

And yes these thighs
Well ,their just to emit more of my sexiness
that I hold
and everyone is afraid of
wire hangers never ignite heat
trust, my flesh is better

And these feet
Soft, beautifully, manicured and groomed are for
kissing
and me walking away
from the nonsense

Of what you consider beauty
I can see my own HALO, hear me !

Well, let me introduce Myself

So you got to understand

There is nothing soft about me

I am durable

And my strength outweighs an army of numerous forces

It is a fine mixture of assertive and aggressiveness that keeps individuals

Guessing in which direction I am going

No there is no gray, cause black and white are my natural hues

That is how you catch the realness rainbow

With a for sure pot of gold, if you understand respect

I demand it

And will ostracize all those who can't keep up

There are rules regulation and principles that I follow

But because of my cardinal I do bleed

My healing comes from the internal

So the external can emit a power from my natural waves

I am a summersault with all the flexibility and
endurance

And at the end of the day

I am a pitcher of water

That satisfies the thirst of all

Say Hello

to the

MOUNTAIN!

You must not Know Bout Me

I hate to be rude
but you don't respect and understand my plight
I put my all in you and you insisted
on continuing to put up a fight

Your secret life
Is always hid
and sure to be kept out of sight
You're the gentlest thing during the day
And you spread your little Ego through the night

But someone should have told you
and you should have listened and learned
that when you play with a woman emotions
It's another "As the world's turns"

You may think you're smart and getting away with
the obvious
But please don't exclude my revenge
and think that it is
because I am jealous

The coming home late
And swearing all the time that you have been with
your homies
But you reek of alcohol and sex and don't
Forget their were pink panties

No need to erase your whore's numbers
Cause fool we share a joint bill
So don't worry about confrontation
cause it is me that is out for the kill

Continue to make your careless moves
Cause every good dog has his day
Don't get scared now ni**a cause
You thought you could dangle it in my face

So as I observe you
and watch your patterns change
And I realize that you are inferior
and selfish
cause you are a human drain

So I carefully planned and calculated
if I really wanted to leave a scar
So yes, I screwed your best friend
And
Busted all the windows out your car!!

You Rise

From the morning when your feet hit the carpet or
wooden floor, you carefully calculate the moments
that will lead you closer to the success of getting out
of the house on time. In order, clothes, food,
breakfast, washed faces, brushed teeth, packed
lunches, homework checked, beds made, house tidy,
car is warmed, 7:45 and you will be on time

You keep that smile on your face because the world
doesn't have to know your hurt or sorrow... the world
doesn't need to know you are living from check to
check... the world doesn't need to know what is
going on with you at all, they can just see the smile,
they can just focus on how well mannered your
children are,
They can notice your soft tone when you respond, and
pay attention to your assertiveness when you want to
get your point across

You are what you are and still
You rise

You take on your job like it is work and
leave it in the 8 to 5
you understand that multitasking is just a corporate
term for not completing a project and shifting it over
to some unfortunate soul…. but not you...
you complete your task, so ever delicately, daily,
done with precision, effectiveness and efficiency...
you are tailored to distinction because you emit
integrity,

the ethic is outstanding and now we one understand
and because all of that…

You rise

And in the evening when you drop off all the
unnecessary luggage of today,
hyper tension, activities, and breeds of demons only
the devil could love..

You pick up your personals, which you carried for
nine months
And you will not except anything less from them
other than a vision or dream that is permanently
imprinted in their head because you have convinced
yourself and them
that, "you will be better than me"

You will sacrifice your life to make a difference and
change circumstance of any generational curse that
inhibits your heart..
You are the maternal strength, you are what gives life

And still you rise
Dinner is cook, bills are paid… house is silenced and
sometime to quiet
because your heart yearns for that love that will
complete the void…

So as you look upon the trifles of life and see the
dismay in others
it is because they have yet to understand their
purpose...

Remember who you are remember what you do
and remember what you did to be here

You rose and you shall continue to rise

Who cares

And so what
If I live on a hill and have a mansion, that is the size
of a stadium

And so what
If I educated myself in all foreign lands and
languages

Who cares
If I am always objective and leave biases at the door

Who cares
If my heart is full of kindness and extracts hate

Don't be bothered
By my six figured job that causes me to be a
workaholic

Forget the fact
That my leadership skills are fair and outstanding

Don't worry about
The fact that I am candid and can look you in the eye
and be assertive

It is none of your business
That as you fight me I am in the moment of loving
you

And so what
If I am self-aware

And so what

If you are in my ear telling me how fine I am

Not to mention you are captivated by my sexiness

Cause I already know

Cause for me being a dime isn't everything

That's why I am

FORT KNOX

Stepping in Pride

Whether my arch be flat, fallen, or steep
I step with pride
I step in peace

I walk and talk in my immediate zone
because it's part of my natural gender
My shoes carry pieces of my diva personality
Causing ignorance to surrender

I understand this land is mans
So I travel lightly and swiftly on my two shields
Yet my beauty is unmistakable, as I tear up the
concrete
In my fashionable tasteful stiletto heels

I am a woman yes all woman and the elements of me
cause great attention,
because without my walk, or my gentle talk, there
would be no man in existence

Yes, I am Woman!

See I give birth, and create trends
Because God gave me a spirit of comfort
Love that is triumph
A sharp turn that could cause traffic to cease

Whether my arch be flat, fallen, or steep
I step with pride
I step in peace

Yes, he asked and God did agree
That companionship was a necessary to complete his
project
He grabbed a rib, and formed a gem
So that man and woman could now connect

A fine wine that is truly unforgettable
Sensual, desirable, sharp, cunning, and unique
And as time passes on and women remain strong
An Incidentally, men still fall to their feet

They are mothers, lovers, sister daughters
Friends, doctors, comforters and can always remain
intact and sweet
You can find them in the kitchen when they are not
one is not looking
Nurturing, creating their family an array of feasts

Whether my arch be flat, fallen, or steep
I step with pride
I step in peace

So let this be a lesson, while you are stepping
That compromises do not always include
Losing yourself,

Take notice and listen, you can have any attention
As long as it enhances your spiritual wealth

It is about submission, perfect condition but not unto
man,
Because he is not, to whom you shift
Or willingly give your hand

Understand your strength show some respect and
remember to always honor him
Because it is he from where your blessing flow and
where your power stems

So grab onto glory share your story
Shake the devils temptations claim your nations
Let out a big exhale, a sigh, and release

Just remember
Whether your arch be flat, fallen, or steep
Always step with pride
So you can walk in peace

Mirror

So if I were Michael I would ask you to start with the
man in the mirror
But we don't need that mirror
For when i see your face I realize that you are my
reflection
An extension of DNA that was replicated with the
intent of us being family
It is within my spirit to be in awe at the site of your
beauty for you are me, and I, am you

My sister my refuge
The spoke and unspoken friendship
In which
I didn't need years to bond
God laid his hand on it before time began
So that our first greeting
Would manifest into glory
Now in this moment I understand why one could
mistake heaven to
Being on earth
Because the blessing of you has put me in the mind of
living in eternity
My sister my friend
My extension to you is love
For you are forever welcomed in my heart

Satisfy My Soul

Please don't you rock my boat
That's what Bob Marley said
As I sway to his rhythmic understandings
Satisfy in my soul
Smell peace as if I saw the everglades
While the wind rushes against my face
As my heart pounds
Listening to
Blues of the birds whistle to

Yesterdays of perfection
Green grass
Trees bowing to God
In the appreciation of life
Satisfy my soul

And coo at the children that play
And adjust their innocence
While embracing their imagination

Shout at the clouds to open up the heavens and allow
the sun to sprinkle
The creator's opulence and omnipotence
Satisfy my soul

Fill my belly with words of virtue
Fold my hands with strength
And save lost souls with mercy and grace
Gently touch timeless thoughts
And bring cognition to the bliss

So please don't you rock my boat
Because I want to do like Marley did
And

Satisfy my Soul

Don't forget...

It was Eve who led Adam to eat the apple

It was Delilah who drove Samson insane

It was Sarah who held Abrahams heart

It was Coretta who helped Martin see his dream

And Betty who stood by her husband by any means necessary

It is your mother that fused the right genes to create you

It is you who hold the key in your hands

It is you who birth and give life

It is you who has forgotten her power!

Sometimes I just need....Neo Soul

Sometimes I just need some neo soul
A little bit of comfort in my natural
No tripping
Silence as I
Listen to the wind as
It hits the
Hues in my skin

As I twist my locks in my fingers
I feel the need to stretch out and absorb the universe
Regain my power
Refuel and allow the energy to coast through the land
to my brothers and sisters

So that we can organize and parade the beauty of our
light
Run circles of advantageous energy in the hearts of
our souls

Remember who we are and what we were

Representation of educators, kings, queen's, doctors, creators, and thinkers
Thriving for better
Willing to rebel against injustices of our brother
Fighting for a cause even in peace
But as the years trapped and co conspired against the visions we once held

We soon forget and tame our complacency
Using excuses, which just demonstrate incompetence
While following guide
And blaming others for our lax of a plan

Remember
There are those who are
Trapped in a Willie lynch syndrome
"If you want to keep something from a nigger put it in a book"
And we wonder why it appears so difficult to recognize
So…

Sometimes I just need some neo soul
A little bit of comfort in my natural
I need to exhale
No tripping

Traveling in my/her History

You see, I started as merely a rib. A rib from a being,
a creation of Gods, which was formed from dust.
From this rib, I evolved, became mother to a nation,
and gave birth to tribes; even through my pains,
sorrows, and disappointments.
They called me Eve.

I skipped through windy gates of time and found my
home in foreign lands where I wore the finest jewels
and had people bow before my feet. I summoned
wars and created destruction while using my beauty
as an underlying crutch to entice the libido of men
who could not resist.
Cleopatra they whispered.

I closed my eyes and found myself in the coldest
winters, challenged my daughters and sisters to gather
and build comfort in which man was allowed to rest.

I wisped through time procreating and blessing the
earth with seeds that spread throughout the universe.
I opened my eyes and landed on the continent of
Europe 1618-1762. You could hear my name:
Queen Elizabeth, Isabella, Anne, or even Catherine.

I felt up for the challenge and wanted to expand my
power through the lands to make my presence known.
I imposed on the boys that I raised to become men I
prepared men to serve their country in our countries
time of need.

I bandaged, nursed wounds, and cleaned the spilt
blood of those that suffered. I smelt death daily and
embraced visual horrors. I endured rape,
discrimination, belittlement, and embarrassment.
Then I decided to do the unthinkable. I enlisted, and
yes, they let me. I sailed the seven seas.
Loretta Perfectus is what they called me as the wind
blew through my hair.
I was perfect because I no longer had to be seen as
just a nurse.

Unfortunately, as I took two steps forward into my
own existence in time, the shameful envy of the lesser
evils attempted to drag me back. I could not speak up
for my rights because I was believed not to have any.

I just ruled a country not even a breath ago and now I
was treated less than a dog. The irony is by man; and
man, is whom I give life. Therefore, I did what I
knew God had intended me to do; I pressed on to
become the woman God intended me to be.

Therefore, in spite of the ugly, I built institutions and
consumed economic wealth even under the jealousy
and torment of my counterparts. They called it a
bank and me the bank president.
Maggie girl you go!

Although some may not find any pride in my
business, I asked my God for repentance, for I was
going to stomp the feeble minded and embrace my
femininity. I became an activist a feminist,
humanitarian a reformer and a menace to some.

Yes, I am Woman!

I dealt with criticism, hate, prejudice, and ignorance.
To me it was just a mountain I was willing travel, for
the remembrance of all my fellow sisters who
endured the fight as I did.

You see we are one in the same. We bear the same
strife's disappointments, and hard aches.
Even as time spends out control, we are still the same
beings that manifest into victorious flowers. Now I
just laugh in the faces of my opponents who attempt
to disable my faith and abilities.

Although time has changed my stature and resilience
has not. Therefore, now I embrace the new titles I
assembled, they call me Teacher, Doctor, Lawyer,
Professor, Judge, Senator, and Governor.
And, in due time,
Madame President.

Walston

Acknowledgments

First, I give honor to my Lord and Savior Jesus Christ from whom all my blessings come. To my mother and father who gave me life. To my two sons Deltan and Dylan. To everyone who have helped me with this process of creating this book. My right hand girl Keya (assistant), Tee-Tee (cousin thank you for the beautiful photo), My logo designer, Reginald Conyard & Aisha Davis (Logo artist). To my fans that constantly support me and show me, love.

Walston

About the Author

Anica Walston is a native of Petersburg, Virginia. This is Anica's second of two poetry books. The first entitled, "To the Little Girl who Love to Dance." Anica has also published her first novel, "Generational Dysfunctions." Anica is currently in the process of writing the sequel to her first novel. She is self-employed and recently created her own company, *Respect the Gender*. Her ultimate goal is to assist people in her community to increase social skills through hands on training, while also providing counseling services for those suffering through addiction and domestic violence.

Anica is in the process of completing her Master's in Counseling Studies. In her spare time, she loves working on her spoken word projects, writing, spending time with her children, and cooking.

All of Anica's poetry books and novels are available on Amazon.com as well as her Respect the Gender Website.

http://www.wix.com/anicawalston/rtg

Walston

Yes, I am Woman!

Walston

www.ingramcontent.com/pod-product-compliance
Lightning Source LLC
Chambersburg PA
CBHW052108090426
42741CB00009B/1719